The Tailor's Three Sons
& Other New York Poems

for my mother

The Tailor's Three Sons
& Other New York Poems

Mara Bergman

Winner of the
Mslexia Poetry Pamphlet
Competition, 2014

SEREN

Seren is the book imprint of
Poetry Wales Press Ltd.
57 Nolton Street, Bridgend, Wales, CF31 3AE

www.serenbooks.com
facebook.com/SerenBooks
twitter@SerenBooks

The right of Mara Bergman to be identified as
the author of this work has been asserted in accordance
with the Copyright, Designs and Patents Act, 1988.

© Mara Bergman 2015

ISBN: 978-1-78172-261-9

A CIP record for this title is available from the British Library.

All rights reserved. No part of this publication may be reproduced,
stored in a retrieval system, or transmitted at any time or by any means,
electronic, mechanical, photocopying, recording or otherwise without
the prior permission of the copyright holder.

The publisher with with the financial assistance of the Welsh Books Council.

Cover Photograph of New York City by the Author.

Printed in Bembo by Grosvenor Group (Print Services) Ltd

Contents

- 7 The Tailor's Three Sons
- 8 Walking Iron
- 9 Edward Hopper on Long Island
- 10 Navigating New York
- 11 Englishman in New York
- 12 East 13th Street *or* How I Met My Husband
- 13 The Summer My Father Died
- 14 Woman in Wells-next-the-Sea
- 15 Judith's Paper Dolls
- 16 Girl With a Pen in Her Hand
- 17 What My Stepdad Liked
- 18 Upright
- 19 The Part Fiona Played
- 20 Flight 800 to Paris
- 21 My New York Uncle on the London–Hastings Train
- 22 Sharon at the Nail Salon
- 23 A Quarter to Eight, New York Time
- 24 Bolthole
- 25 Special
- 26 Lagoon
- 27 Trying to Kill Time at JFK

- 28 *Acknowledgements*

The Tailor's Three Sons

Nights I can't sleep, I think about the tailor's
three sons and how twelve people lived and worked
in a three-room apartment meant for four when
the Lower East Side was the most crowded place

on the planet. What was it they did? The cutting or basting
or sewing, right here, the finishing or pressing over there
while the clock's heavy ticking kept them sane, insane?
Afternoons they'd elbow through the teeming streets to catch

some air, some news, but after a long day, what else had they
to look forward to but a bowl of soup and then to sleep
on the red velvet sofa which looked, from a distance,
more lavish, and though cherished, was so narrow

it is hard to imagine enough room for even one young boy
to sit down. I think of the sons because when night came
at last, and the whirr of machines had flown out the window,
the clock's ticking rocking like a lullaby, they would

lay down their heads side by side on the sofa,
rest their throbbing feet on wooden chairs and lie, suspended,
to sleep the sleep of the young and the exhausted,
dreaming their immigrant dreams in thin air.

Walking Iron

High above commuters clutching cardboard cups of coffee,
    stepping off curbs, losing hats to the wind, visible/

invisible as any angel among the clouds and spires, spikes
    and wire, floating on air amid the endless high-risers

a man walks iron, believing or not believing in the proverbial
    gift for heights, maybe simply striving to keep fear at bay

if only for his family hundreds of miles away across
    the border. His father's great-grandfather was the first

to leave *Kahnawake*, the Place of the Rapids, to work
    iron and build a bridge across the St Lawrence

and that man's son was first to boom out, to straddle air
    and girders, hoist beams and hammer, it's in

their blood. Their nation built the Empire State, the Chrysler –
    hell, and the most magnificent Towers of all. And after

the disaster, passed on the baton to sons and nephews,
    nieces too, to dismantle the rubble, do what they could.

On Fridays he leaves his four-story walk-up
    in Sunset Park, Brooklyn, but not before stopping

at the Cheesecake Factory or his favourite Manhattan bakery,
    then crosses New York State to another country.

boom out – Mohawk expression for leaving the reservation to work in the city.

Edward Hopper on Long Island

He left the neon-lit cafés and deserted stations
for a winter of snow, mounds of it,
steeped on decks through a neighbourhood
where he didn't know a soul.
He had given up city lights, city life,
to see the sun rise from a corner of a garden,
a flock of geese pummel across clouds.
At last the chance to study the filaments
of a squirrel's tail, the shock of red cardinal.
He'd go to bed later and later,
wake up earlier until
there was no discernible difference
between darkness and light.
Three a.m., looking out on the snow
when a plane passed over the row of split-
levels, he spotted that thin divide
where streetlight met houselight – light
on the side of a building his favourite thing.
Maybe he wasn't so far from his life,
maybe it was then he stopped questioning
what he was doing amid the snowlight
and a pale orange glow
over the telephone wire, heat steaming.

Navigating New York

It doesn't hit me until I'm strolling back in the too-grey light,
sauntering, trucking, speed-walking along Fifth Avenue,

then Sixth, over to Forty-something Street,
and for a second I get a whiff and a breath and a look

at signs, windows, buildings stretching up and up.
I'm in my stride, the rhythm of me and the city.

Forty-second, Forty-first, the years are rolling back
and I'm returning home from work, to our apartment in Brooklyn,

our brownstone on Henry Street. *Remind me why we left?*
The smell of semolina bread, the deli that sold baked mozzarella

like fat balls of fudge, the restaurants along Atlantic Avenue,
low green lights and Arab music. And what about that birthday

you bought me the Nutshell Library and a book of Elizabeth Bishop
at the shop on Court? Admit it: we were happy.

And weren't we like everyone else on Sunday mornings,
strolling about the promenade, all of New York at our shoulder?

Lights change and I cross as the red hand of God
gives way to the figure escaping.

The sky is thickening grey and greyer, one drop follows another.
gigantic raindrops, then *flash!* –

sheets of rain pour over us. We detour through Macy's
handbags and perfumes, come out through men's shirts

where shoppers huddle by revolving doors, drenched and waiting.
We take a deep breath, ready for the home stretch, then dash

to Penn Station, crossing rivers, whole oceans.

Englishman in New York

for J.G.

You rescued him from the dark
    subway platform as a train heading downtown

pulled into the station, he was something rare
    you wanted. Your fingers lit his elbow

and guided him in. After that, dinners in Little
    Italy, India, Korea, then his apartment,

its furniture and walls all beige, with dozens
    of photographs, he described every one, painting

the ideal English childhood before his eyes
    clouded over. His acute sense

of order, the shirts and ties and suits
    coordinated in his closet, one drawer for blue socks, one

for black, his fingers caressing every surface, expert
    at wielding a knife. At night his accent

cut the New York City air, *Why have a dog
    when a stick would do?*, and with it he tap, tap

tapped into your heart. When you made love
    his eyes were utter blue.

East 13th Street *or* How I Met My Husband

If Aunt Dorothy and Uncle Seymour had moved
    out of their two-bedroom apartment with my four cousins
as planned, I never would have met Susan Silver,
    who lived in their courtyard, Utopia Parkway, Queens,
and grew up with Sharon and Tara, and years later
    I might not have known her at university
or become best friends, lived together in that red semi
    on East Street next to Feeney's Fine Foods and Drink
with Marla, the actress who spent weekends in New York City
    with a jazz musician twice her age. The three of us
ate only with chopsticks at a cable spool we used as a table,
    visited Dunkin' Donuts in the middle of the night
and found, once, a star on our receipt and won
    another dozen. We lived up the street from Mary and Albert
with their parakeets, Sonya and Raskolnikov, and Peter the potter,
    who borrowed my Brother typewriter to write a book
on Abstract Expressionism. I would never have heard
    that Susan met an English guy that summer while camping
with her boyfriend in Vermont, that he would borrow a sleeping bag
    and have to return it. She would not have rung me up
to join her in Manhattan, and I would not have said no and
    she would not have cajoled me until she convinced me to go.
I would not have seen him standing in the doorway
    of his friend's apartment on East 13th Street and thought *Yes*.

The Summer My Father Died

Boys stoned frogs the summer my father died,
surrounded the stream, there was never any hope,
and followed the floating white bellies.

My sister and I were left there, in Accord, New York,
in a bungalow swarming with cousins.
We wanted to be like them, unaware

of our steps as we ran through the dark grass.
Or of night's enormity – all those beautiful stars
forgotten above the wooden roofs.

Our aunts lived windows apart
and our uncles wore those white undershirts
with the scooped-out neck and arms.

On porch steps, as the orange light collected moths,
Aunt Dorothy kissed us goodbye, unable to answer
questions we couldn't ask.

At home, lilacs and roses still bloomed under my window.
Nose pressed against the screen, I longed to hear
my parents' voices murmuring in the garden.

Woman in Wells-next-the-Sea

Wearing thick black shoes, she steps straight out of the Bronx,
walks past the storefronts in her long white coat,

shuffling like my Grandma Eva along Olinville Avenue
when she'd take us to the candy store for bunches of lollipops

wrapped in polka-dots, or the playground's grey cement
with its swings of stainless steel chained to the sky.

My sister and I called her every Friday before sundown –
Olinville 4-8033 – and saw her once a month

on Sundays, her building smelling of chicken soup,
the black and white tiles of her bathroom floor

shaped like lozenges, like chicken wire. One room
led to another in her railroad apartment by the El,

whole rooms shook when a train passed overhead
or the girl upstairs thundered on roller skates

across the living-room ceiling. My grandmother
hid twenty-dollar bills between pages of Dickens

she never read, one by one lost everything – country,
husband, two grandsons and then my father

and Uncle Harry, – her sadness the swelling violins
playing "Tara's Theme" at the end of The Million Dollar Movie

each time we got ready to leave, everything turning black
and white, the bridge bathed in diamonds, the thick Bronx night.

Judith's Paper Dolls

I used to confuse her with Anne Frank,
    my cousin Judith. Something about their smile
and dark eyes, the way their thick hair held
    so much life. I can still see her

in our grandmother's apartment
    writing words I didn't understand, later
folding sheets of paper and cutting out rows
    of children holding hands. For years — decades —

she went missing, the one and only cousin
    on my father's side, and after Uncle Harry died
she married an Italian boy and fled across the border.
    If only we had stayed in touch

we would be sisters now, releasing secrets
    behind doors of that narrow railroad apartment,
flooding rooms with light as each El train
    clattered past, rattling the windows.

Girl With a Pen in Her Hand

That Saturday I lay in bed, head throbbing,
throat on fire, my stepdad chose it
from the library, a biography

about three sisters who lived somewhere
in England. I loved to read
how they loved to write, I wanted to be

a sister like that. If it had been another day,
if I'd not had another throbbing throat…
I'm searching for it now, remembering

how I lay there turning pages
as the pain began to ease, releasing me
into winter on some windy heath.

What My Stepdad Liked

He liked his eggs soft and he loved all fruits
though peaches were his favourite. For family barbecues

he cut watermelon into baskets and scooped out the balls
of flesh. He took a gourmet cooking class at the temple

and perfected a chicken dish with spinach,
introduced me to cherryneck clams at Ehrhart's

and my friend Susan to steamers. He went out fishing
from Port Jefferson and had his picture taken

next to a six-foot tuna, camped with the Boy Scouts,
enjoyed long drives round the Island

when gas was cheap. He and my mother had a social life
I envied: dinners, theatre, long walks up Fifth Avenue

and down Park, then trips abroad, though they never went
on safari as planned. He drove from New York to Florida

with a tumour the size of an apple, read whole novels
in the bath, saw his grandchildren grow up halfway.

Upright

She's ninety, or older,
and should stand against the opposite wall
to avoid radiators or drafts from the door
and as she's probably thirsty
a coffee can of water at the base of her strings
should ease her (though I've never seen a coffee can
in England). Because she's not overstrung
but strung straight, and her highest octave
has all new strings, silver threads
wound round their pegs that flash, like fillings,
he will try his very best to keep her
in tune. But structurally she's unsound,
he calls her damaged. Damaged!
The crack behind her soundboard
quite serious. But to me
she is lovely – a lustrous brown
with pale wood inlay and mother-of-pearl
she has the dignity of my grandmother
who lived to a hundred and four. And if she stays in tune
while the tuner is here, she may pull through.
We must treat her with care, not move her
(though my grandmother moved from New York
to Florida at the age of ninety-four) or bang her keys
the way my sister did in high school, though I'm sure
no one will ever play her the way
my stepdad played, his entire body bouncing,
his hands bursting with show tunes.

The Part Fiona Played

She lived down the corridor, or we thought she did,
but maybe that was only DeLea. He was older,
wore glasses, his voice was high-pitched
and they partied to Springsteen at all hours.

Littell Hall, Oneonta, New York, and this girl
from somewhere in England.
She wore skirts that flounced when she danced –
and she always danced first, had every boy swooning

though DeLea had already nabbed her.
We never really spoke, but she was my first
English person up close, fitting in
without even trying. She skipped classes, was always

hung over, but things somehow went right,
her accent gloriously spilling
while the rest of us struggled with work and love,
the long winter days full of snow up the hill,

hair freezing those nights after swimming, arms aching
with loss. Last I heard she was living in California
and never looks back.

Flight 800 to Paris

I wake to news of fireballs
breaking the sky, the sea a swell of smoke,

and I think of my parents on Long Island,
stepping out on their deck smelling disaster –

smouldering fuselage, cloth, skin.
I think of me packing in the basement

the summer I came to England,
forcing my belongings into the two cases

for the journey. The room was cool,
the freezer hummed and the light was the grey

of the ceiling, oppressive and secure. Outside,
grass browned, and from the moment of take-off

emerged a new beginning. I think of those students,
and their parents daring to watch, proud

and full of fear, as they packed while practising French,
already feeling a difference in themselves.

My New York Uncle
on the London-Hastings Train

He's over there, halfway
down the carriage of the train,
the left side of his face
in the aisle, the other
obscured by the fabric of the seat,
blue and slashed with dashes.
He wears pale blue under grey
and through black-rimmed glasses
looks down beyond his black moustache
to read the evening paper –
so much like my mother's younger brother
I want to run and ask him,
What on earth are you doing here?
What about my aunt and cousins
and your business on Steinway Street
in Queens? And without a doubt
he would take me back
to the diner on Ditmars Boulevard
with its seashore décor and its jukebox
drowning out the subway.

Then I see the other half
of his face, the half that clearly says
this man is younger, that together
the two don't add up.
There is no light
in this man's eyes.
And he gets up too soon.
And he looks straight at me
and hasn't even the grace
to fake a smile.

Sharon at the Nail Salon

Every Wednesday without fail, despite
her treatments at the hospital, my cousin Sharon
travelled to the nail salon her sister ran in Little Neck,
Queens, above buses and banks, streams
of shoppers, and entered the calm of music
and footbaths, cuticles softening, callouses
lovingly scraped clean, all that dead skin falling
like snow, like the rest of her life when she went there.
With lavender and rose, feet and hands were massaged new.
Afterwards, a woman with a Russian accent
would bring a tray of bottles lined up like sweets.
She chose Hot Red each time, my cousin
who used to chew her nails worse than I chewed mine.
Long, slow brushstrokes the brightness of berries, of balloons.

A Quarter to Eight, New York Time

A quarter to eight and the sun streaming in.
    In my life across the Atlantic, the day half gone already,

my children having lunch, the light a little stronger.
    Here, I have no children, husband, house, no work

to go to. I wear jeans ripped at the knees, my hair's unruly
    and I'm for ever dreaming of someplace better.

On my shelf is an oversize paperback, *Vagabonding in America*.
    I read it every night, sleep in an orange mummy bag

I haven't yet shared, my windows open to the whistle of trains
    heading west. I plan to cram the things I can

into the bicycle panniers I made from a Frostline kit and cross
    America with a friend I haven't yet fallen in love with,

who won't be the one to leave me on a corner in New York City.
    That rush of cars up the road in the rain

is always with me. Seventeen and full of hope,
    heading somewhere.

Bolthole

I would return to Brooklyn and live as near the bridge as I could.
Keep a cat, have a garden, be on a first name basis
with the man at the newsstand and the woman at the bakery
who serves strong coffee and sweet poppy-seed cake.
Each day I would journey by subway to Manhattan,
work high up in a skyscraper on Park Avenue,
meet friends afterwards for drinks at one of those
outdoor places with tables that stretch to the curb
and sit under an umbrella as the sun's going down.
I'd have my hair cut by Richard, and on Saturdays
do my laundry at the Laundromat on Henry Street,
visit my mother on Long Island, changing trains
at Jamaica. I'd be a regular at the local cinema
and trattoria by the promenade, where you'd find me
every Sunday reading the *New York Times*
on a bench overlooking the East River.

Special

for Martin

We talk about packing up
to live where we did before the children,
the dogs and cats and apple trees, grass
crying to be cut. The bookshop is still here,
the cinema and bakeries, all the delis we knew.
I've waited to come back in winter with you,

the air pure cold, and bright.
We pass the promenade's verandahs
and terracotta, the city a mere stone's throw
across the river, and imagine
spending lunchtimes at the Cobble Hill Diner,
choosing from the menu's daily specials.

Lagoon

for Jean Schuster (1921-1996)

As if you could take a patch of light
and place it on water – spotlight

of moonlight, rippling lagoon-light
the silence of egret, of heron.

I have carried it along the eastern seaboard
from a lake in upstate New York, where

children watched fires in summer,
ran barefoot under shooting stars,

and from a wood in Massapequa, Long Island,
at the bend before traffic lights,

children bicycled in straw hats, balanced
fishing rods across handlebars,

imagined the Mississippi. Eventually
it alights here, where palm trees

adorn either bank, though in darkness
only the fiery ripples can be seen

dancing and dancing, as if
they could ever extinguish themselves.

Trying to Kill Time at JFK

I am earlier than I've ever been before, for anything,
breeze through check-in, am free
to wander the concourse of duty-free and places to eat –
Wok 'n' Roll, McDonald's, muffins at Ritazza, sandwiches
at Au Bon Pain, and gallons of coffee, coffee everywhere,
as if caffeine were the secret ingredient of flight.
At the Museum Shop, I study calendars, mugs, keyrings,
imagine a stranger begging me to choose something – anything –
and without hesitation, I point at the citrine earrings under glass
with their fine Victorian clasps. One whole hour
                                                at Hudson Bookshop
perusing dedications, measuring what I haven't read,
then comparing candy displays at Hudson News
among hundreds of magazines. *What could be better
than having a back massage at the Xpress Spa?*
I visit the bathroom every half hour,
check my hair, redden my lips, drink from the taller of two
                                                water fountains
before standing in front of Longchamps Luggage and Handbags,
before going outside into the air of New York City
one last time to watch a sparrow, listen to traffic on wide lanes
for what might be a very long time, for what may be for ever.

Acknowledgements

Thanks are due to the editors of the publications in which some of these poems first appeared:

Acumen, Ambit, Internazionale (Rome), *Poetry London Newsletter, Poetry Review, The Frogmore Papers, The North*, anthologies *Buzz, Pique* and *Solitaire* (Templar) and *May Day* (Cinnamon Press). "The Summer My Father Died" won a prize in the Kent and Sussex Poetry Society Open Competition; "East 13th Street *or* How I Met My Husband" won a prize in the Troubadour Poetry Competition 2012. The title poem was inspired by a visit to the Tenement Museum in New York City.

I would also like to thank my writer friends Susan Wicks, Caroline Price, Mary Gurr, Moniza Alvi and Suzanne Cleary for their insightful comments and continued support. Thanks, as ever, to my husband, Martin Camus-Smith, and our children, Marissa, Eva and Jonathan, as well as Amy Wack and Jamie Alexander Hill at Seren and Debbie Taylor and Robyn Henderson at *Mslexia*.